VOICES

MW00942795

Women's Journeys of Listening Within

by

Stephanie Petrie

ALSO BY STEPHANIE PETRIE

*Following the Signs: One Woman's Journey for
Happiness, Meaning, and a Quest for a Spiritual Life*

Cover Design: Carrie House, HOUSEdesign llc
Interior Design: Kurt Lancaster

To my mother with heartfelt gratitude for
all her love and support

ACKNOWLEDGEMENTS

They say it takes a village to raise child, and I believe it is true as well with a book. Many special people have helped me over the years in the writing of this project, and I am profoundly grateful for their presence in my life.

With heartfelt thanks and loving gratitude to my dear friend, advisor, and mustang yogi, Janna Jones for believing in this project from the very beginning, encouraging and supporting me to write about women and their intuition. Your loving guidance, wisdom and generosity of spirit have contributed so much to the book.

Thank you to my committee chairpersons Julie Schutten and Jon Torn, I am deeply grateful for your encouragement and guidance throughout the project.

For all of the women who gave so much of themselves in telling their brave stories, you inspire me with your hearts and wisdom. I am so grateful for the sharing of your life stories and entrusting me to write about them. You are the brightest of lights creating a path for others.

With deepest thanks and appreciation to all my friends for their encouragement, support and love: Lisa Adams, Jeremy Adair, Sanjam Ahluwalia, Shawn Akard, Claire Akard, Sherri Akard, Peter Bals, Liz Bohlke, Maria Bond, Liz Bush, Tracey Carney, Karen Carrozza, Nicole Williams-Chambers, Patti Decoursey, Hilary Dumitrescu, Sesa Edgar, Diane Ewing, Cara Wilson Granat, Carrie House, Michelle Iavicolli, May Sheppard Ketchner, Maia Kincaid, Ellen Kozub, Beau L'Amour, Suzanne Lovvorn, Cher Lynn, Kathryn and Martin Moller, Manna Moller, Sienna Moller, Laura Moser, Alison Pelose, Jennifer Rolley, Laura Gray-Rosendale, Lenka Studnicka, Mary Tolan, Carolyn Young.

For two of the most beautiful yoga teachers Joni Haug, and Erin Widman with her studio the Yoga Experience in Flagstaff, AZ—you have both always uplifted me body and soul with your soulful teachings for more than a decade and I am so grateful for your loving care. And Joni, you are a body healer extraordinaire!

For Tessie and Kelly McCabe, amazing teachers and musicians, loving thanks and heartfelt appreciation for all of your support and belief in me, your light shines so brightly, and I am so grateful for your presence in my life.

For all the women in the Flagstaff Book Club for your love and support, and beautiful cooking with soulful conversations.

A loving thank you to my family for all their encouragement: Bobbie Mattison and Dave Savage; Bill Mattison and Brett Blyshak; Judy Bennett; Lorie Mattison; William, Dalia and Nora Mattison—especially sweet Nora, who lights up the world with her smile.

To my son Morgan for being so understanding with all the time spent on my computer and for his amazing growth into the special person that he is; to my husband Kurt, for his unconditional love and support, you have been my steady rock and I cherish you.

TABLE OF CONTENTS

PREFACE

Learning to use my intuition is part of my spiritual journey, a process that continues to unfold. I've had days when I trusted everything, and others when my trust disappeared, and I felt vulnerable, scared and alone. One of the hardest lessons I've learned in trusting my own inner voice is the need to relinquish control of the outcome of any given situation and trust that all is well. Trust that I'm doing the best that I can. Trust that my best is not always the same each day. Trust that I am loved and supported on my journey. Trust that the angels and archangels, my guides and teachers are always around me. Trust that when I hear messages for other people it is okay to share those messages with them. Trust in my own unlimited inner resources and that God is always with me. Trust that my infinite creative possibilities will translate into fully supporting my household. Trust that the universe is kind, loving and generously supportive of my efforts to grow and be all that I imagine myself to be.

The gradual gaining of trust in myself is an ongoing journey of soul development that requires me to reach beyond what I know and believe that Spirit is the wisdom to guide me. When we allow ourselves to be guided by our own intuitive knowings—the self doubt and fear in our decision makings drop away, and our lives become richer and fuller. It doesn't happen all at once. There isn't a magic switch that gets turned on and then our lives become immediately different. But, as the awareness in ourselves changes, our consciousness changes too, and becomes more in tune with the greater good of all. As we trust in our intuition, the deeper mysteries of life become clearer. Intuition is our guide into a more loving relationship with ourself and others.

Our intuition is authentic. There is nothing fake here; it is the part of us that is guiding, nudging us into areas of our lives to be explored. Intuition is our connection to the divine. It is the compass that tells us when we walk into a room full of people who we are drawn to. It allows us to make better choices in all aspects of life. Intuition is self-guided. It is our beacon to take us from one point to the next.

Our intuition reassures us that there are few wrong choices. A turning point in my life was when I learned to trust my inner voice, when I understood that this goodness is always accessible to me. Of course part of the richness and difficulty of my life is that there is so much that remains unknown, but I have faith in the unconditional love of the universe. Though I face life's numerous challenges each day, I have learned to rely on the love and support of my intuition, which often comes to me by way of the angels and other teachers. They have given me the courage to open up and trust in the universe.

Growth can be very uncomfortable, especially when we crack the foundations that we've built up over time. The desire for growth and change pushes us forward.

When we acknowledge, embrace and allow our intuition to grow, our lives can blossom in ways we cannot imagine. We have so much wisdom at our calling, wisdom that lies within, just waiting to be birthed.

This calming mantra from the Christian mystic, Julian of Norwich (1342 –1416) says it so gracefully:

> *All shall be well, and all shall be well,*
> *and all manner of things be well …*

INTRODUCTION

As a child I had always talked to God. My family was not particularly religious; in fact church was more perfunctory around the holidays and religion rarely discussed at home. It was not unusual for me to be in my room alone talking aloud to an imagery playmate who happened to be God. I remember closing my eyes, taking a deep breath, and talking to God, the universe, angels, whoever would hear me, and then sitting quietly listening for a response.

When I was 10, an older friend who was 12 taunted me explaining to me that she was going to tell a boy that I had a crush on him, and that I watched him walk home from school every day. I was frantic, thinking the world was going collapse around me and the life I knew would be over. I locked myself in the bathroom, sat on the toilet and prayed out loud to God and the angels, with tears streaming down my face. Suddenly the air around me seemed to still; I felt absolute peace, and I knew that everything would be fine. While I don't remember the exact words from that day, the "knowing" that everything would be okay has stayed with me and has translated into an intuitive guidance that is now commonplace but remains extraordinary.

It has not been an easy road. Throughout my childhood there were other instances of knowing, that made me feel like an outsider. I pushed back this part of myself as I entered high school because I was eager to fit in. My intuition was always hovering around, but it was not terribly hard to ignore. In college, I listened to the voices of society to help determine my life path. If I had listened to my intuition a life more in sync with my passions would have undoubtedly opened up for me.

I married when I was 24, and my intuition was still waiting on the sidelines for me. Nothing in the marriage worked after the first few years, and I recognized it was time to end the relationship. My intuition repeatedly told me to close the door and another would open.

I knew the marriage was not going to last, but for divorce to become my reality was another matter entirely. My self-confidence plummeted, diminished to almost nothing. I walked around our house after the divorce, feeling empty and entirely disoriented. I remember sitting in front of the kitchen window asking out loud what my next steps should be. On a bookshelf, I spotted a poetry book I had not read before. They were illuminating poems about women and nature. I closed my eyes and focused on my life—concentrating on a new road that would open up and take me where it may.

If I had not followed my intuition that nudged me to grab that poetry book, the defining moment that shaped the next part of my life may have been lost. It was hard to pay attention at first, but the more questions I asked and the more I listened it became easier and easier to tune in to my intuition that was clearly prodding me forward. I did most of my thinking in the kitchen, but later at sunset I would walk on the beach and then sit on the sand watching the waves. The rhythmic movement of the water put me into a meditative state, and I felt peaceful listening to the call of the gulls. Ideas for a new life began flooding into my mind. I started watching for signs around me for clues as to where I would need to go. Sedona, Arizona came up frequently in conversations from strangers, ads on television, and at a visit to a local bookstore that was running a DVD about Sedona. Following my intuition and the many signs, I soon took a trip to Arizona, a state that I had never been to before.

The red mountains surrounding Sedona seemed to beckon me. The smells of the desert and night air cleansed my soul. *I felt at home.* My visit there opened me up to an entirely new landscape, and because I felt so comfortable there, I knew it was my next destination. The move to Arizona from my home in California happened entirely because I listened to intuition and the signs, and then followed through with actions on it. I didn't know a soul in Arizona at the time, but I believed in the wisdom that was coming from inside of myself rather than listening to information gained from outside sources, no matter how well-intentioned.

After the move to Arizona, I followed my intuition again to take a trip to Germany to visit with my best friends, Shawn and Bruce. While there, Shawn gave me a birthday gift of a week in Egypt. I had a life-changing event while traveling to Egypt visiting the King's Chamber in the Pyramid of Giza. I was chanting in the King's Chamber and felt a shaft of energy enter through my head and I passed out cold on the floor. I believe part of me died in that instant and a new part of me emerged when I awakened. My intuition became alarmingly intense once I came home from Egypt, as I could now "hear" messages from people's guides. Guides are souls that accompany us on our life journeys. They can be angels, deceased family members, or members of your soul family that are committed to your growth.

My heightened sense of intuition literally and figuratively knocked me out at first. I had been rendered unconscious in the King's Chamber; and then when I began acknowledging my intuition, new opportunities began happening for me at breath-taking speed. When I view my life before and after trusting and using intuition, there is no contest which way of life I prefer. My intuition has become my internal compass guiding me in all sorts of situations—meeting new people, going back to school, scheduling an air flight, or maintaining my health.

As productive and liberating as intuitive life may be, it has never found an easy home in most people's lives. Carl E. Jung defines intuition as "perception via the unconscious" (1921:

528). He was one of the first scholars and researchers to define intuition, and ninety years later there is still no general agreement among researchers as to its exact definition. Transpersonal psychologist Frances Vaughan defines it as a "… knowing without being able to explain what we know" (1979: 46). In our society where such a high value is placed on what is tangible, intuition is rarely valued as a legitimate decision-making tool or resource.

Mona Lisa Schulz writes in *The New Feminine Brain* (2005) that women's brains have been essentially rewired, due to having had to "… 'fit' their brains into a male world…[we've] had to learn how to, as the song says, 'walk like a man' and 'talk like a man,' but stay a woman inside (p. 3). The importance of intuition, Schulz explains is "the ability to make good, beneficial, or correct decisions with insufficient information." She states that, "We women today need to appreciate our intuition, which has sometimes been denigrated by our culture … intuition helps us to learn to adapt and to what the world demands of us" (p. 8).

Over time, with trial and error, I have found it much easier to trust in what I know instead of giving away that power to others. Have you had instances of knowing what was right in any given moment, then doubted that information, only to be shown moments later if you had followed that initial awareness it would have been a better course of action? I learned after so many instances that trusting my intuition is the best option for me. It took a long time for me to understand, but it does not have to take a long time for you. You need only to trust your intuition, which has been beckoning and waiting for you to integrate into the fabric of your life. The threads that connect you to your own knowing, the purposeful piece inside of you that relies on your acknowledgment of this awareness is a breath away. Releasing those voices of old is liberating and necessary. Releasing those old ties that bind you to a past of false expectations frees you. Allowing your intuition to unfold, and giving *yourself permission* to use it and validate it is empowering.

Using my intuition and speaking to many people has shown me that everybody has access to intuitive guidance. You were born with intuition. Once you begin to acknowledge your intuition and then integrate it into your daily life, doors will begin to open and opportunities that you may never have thought possible will become available to you. Many of the women's stories I tell in this book show their heartfelt struggles as they grew deeper into the wisdom of acknowledging their own voice. It takes courage and guts to change, but once you decide to live a life guided by your intuition and your own knowing—the magic begins to flow.

I took a step forward, then another and trusted that all would be well. When you start a life all over again, the newness and unfamiliarity of the landscape can be daunting. But, the rewards for being your own authentic self far outweigh going back to live from a past that no longer serves your highest good. The sense of freedom from listening to your own heart is the first step to understanding the new road ahead of you.

This book contains stories of my lived experiences, and the personal experiences of the twelve women who have graciously agreed to be interviewed. They have given freely of their hearts and time in order to share their own experiences of intuition. I am profoundly grateful for the opportunity to bear witness to their personal and professional stories. They are a source of inspiration to me, and I hope they will be for you as well.

Breathe, open up your heart and soul and
read these women's courageous stories.

CHAPTER ONE

Discernment and Trust

~~

My Story

I began hearing voices after my return from Egypt and the experience I had in the King's Chamber in the Great Pyramid of Giza. At the time, I believed that I had passed out cold on the floor in the King's chamber, but actually I had a Near Death Experience (NDE). On New Year's Eve day, I came home to Sedona and began an amazing journey of trust and faith that continues to unfold. The evening I returned from Egypt, my friend and I did a meditation to bring in the New Year with love and healing. During the meditation a voice spoke through me, and introduced herself as an angel. It felt as if I stepped aside to allow the angel to speak thorough me, but I was fully present aware of my surroundings. Part of my consciousness moved to the left side of my body, and there was a physical sensation in that part of my body. My head opened up, and energy came into me through my crown chakra at the top of my head. I let the "me" step aside and I acted as the spiritual conduit.

My friend saw my face change as the angel began speaking, and she heard everything the angel said. Sara was a Reiki healer, and not unfamiliar with channeling. But, this was a brand new experience for me! This expansion of self, happened to me 20 years ago. In the months following my trip to Egypt I met weekly with Sara to practice my "sessions" with angels. Eventually people's guides also spoke through me. It was hard, hard work. At the end of these sessions my body would be limp, and I felt as if I had run a marathon. The muscles in my face ached from the vocal patterns and mannerisms that weren't familiar to me. I would drive home and just lie on the floor until I could function again. I did feel supported and deeply loved, but my body went through a myriad of changes. I also changed my diet and became a vegetarian. I spent more time in nature and near water. I wrote in a journal each morning outlining my thoughts as soon as I awoke, and I joined a women's group for creative writing. The journal writing helped to center me for the day and continues to inspire me to go deeper into myself. I cried and emptied myself out, only to cry some more.

I kept at it and experimented each week with the energy. I questioned myself constantly and definitely was not trusting in the process. It was like pulling teeth without anesthesia. And I still had to wake up each morning and engage everyday aspects of living. At the time I felt it was mundane, but looking back, I see this was a blessing, and the glue that held me together. I believe our daily acts set up a framework that help us go out into the world as our best selves which enables us to listen to our intuition, and live a life with happiness and peace.

Initially, when working with the guides and angels, I was extremely sensitive to electricity. Televisions shorted out around me, computer screens went off, and light bulbs flickered in my home. One afternoon, I was walking out of the grocery store with a bag of groceries in each hand. I walked toward my car and saw a man with jumper cables on his car battery. I knew this was going to be a problem. I walked closer to my car and heard him yell, "Start it up," to someone in the other car. I "felt" the electricity running through the cables. My arms flew up in the air and the groceries went flying everywhere as my body convulsed with the power of the electricity running through the cables. I fell to the ground near the car clutching my sides, and as soon as the person stopped revving his car engine, I stopped my convulsing. The man ran over, helped me get up and pick up the groceries, and then I walked shakily to my car. I sat in the parking lot for quite a while and then drove the short distance home.

I was angry it happened. Angry with myself and angry at the world of spirit for letting it happen to me. Later that week I had a similar experience. Traveling to the east coast, I was at the airport walking through the metal detectors and my arms began moving around jerkily. I felt the energy course through me. As I walked through the airport I was conscious of many people's thoughts. I could hear bits of what they were thinking as I walked by them, information bombarded me, and I wondered how I could exist in this state and remain sane.

I was also deeply depressed. I wondered what people would think when they found out about me. Would they think I was crazy? Along with all of these new experiences I had many questions that kept cropping up. Who do I tell? How do I *trust* what's coming from me will be genuinely helpful to other people? For the first year I kept to myself, wondering what was going to happen next. One day, fed up, I decided to make a change. I took a firm stance and planted my feet, shouting at the sky waving my hands around. I had always prayed as a child to God or Spirit and thought of her as a divine force that watched over us. My relationship with Spirit is intimate, and there were no barriers to how I talked to her. It's always been as if I was conversing with a best sister friend:

> *Ok God, this is too much. The energy is not settling into my body, I can't go through life with my body so sensitive to energy. Please tone it down for me so I can feel comfortable living here! I don't know what I'm supposed to do with all of this, but help me out!*

My body's sensitivity to energy lessened considerably over time. I learned how to work with my body and intuit anything out of the ordinary with the environment. Slowly, I began to feel joy and wonder at the unfolding events that were happening. It was as if a cocoon had cracked open around my body, fallen off, and I felt lighter than I ever had in my body and spirit. I felt pushed out of my own way and began speaking to people as an Intuitive, channeling their guides and angels. Rarely am I put in a situation where I walk up to a complete stranger and say, "Hi, I have a message for you...". In the small number of times that it has happened in my life—I just delivered the message with love through a casual conversation.

I quickly realized that many people do not believe in energy work and channeling. At first, in my excitement I was not sensitive to others and their beliefs. But I learned over time to be patient, to stay in the moment and watch for the signs that are an important part of my unfolding reality. I didn't push anything, and I stopped insisting that I had to know all the answers to my questions immediately. I began to feel a freedom in my reality that was not present before. It felt as if for the first time I could breathe and have access to a world of information that was coming from inside of me. I felt the integrity of being open to whatever was going to happen in the moment and a peaceful acceptance of my life.

I've gotten more confident about myself. I've learned that I don't have to worry about what I say when I am channeling. I'm discerning, I trust, and I've allowed myself to not have an attachment to the outcome. It's from a space of deep love. The angels and guides express a profound love for the person for whom I am channeling—I feel that their love is an incredible healing force. When I channel for clients, I truly never know what's going to come out of my mouth, but I am confident that it will be loving and uplifting. Guides and angels from the spiritual realm will often share strategies to help my clients overcome a problem they are experiencing. Sometimes the guides and angels urge my clients to pursue the dreams they have forgotten about. They provide people with steps to get closer to making their dreams a reality. Sometimes the people who come to me are living and working without passion and focus. They're just living and checking the boxes of their daily to do list. Rather than listening to their hearts, they have taken life paths that others thought were best for them. They've put themselves in a place where their own gifts and strengths are not acknowledged. The core issue comes back to believing in themselves and what really makes them happy. If you can get back to that basic and important part of living, acknowledging what gives you joy— then the opportunities come to you to make that so in your life.

It has taken me a long time to learn to trust my intuition. I have learned to use my body for guidance. If I'm around a person, for example, and I start to feel drained, then I need to walk away and recharge. If it happens several times, then I likely need to reevaluate that relationship. If the relationship feels like an even exchange of giving and taking, then I walk away with my energy intact and uplifted. If I feel misgivings in my body from the relationship, I wait for a time and the answer for the cause of the misgivings will be revealed to me. Usually I want to know right away, but waiting will reveal more of a truth about the situation. No judgments. Trust, trust, and then more trust.

While writing this book towards the end of the summer, I lived briefly in the middle of the desert at a small artist community. One evening after working I walked down to dinner, and returning back to my room on a rough dirt road, a large animal loomed ahead of me. I carried a flashlight, and when I turned the beam on ahead of me, a mountain lion stared back unblinkingly. Her eyes glowed golden with the light. I froze, then became calm as the cat leapt off the road and down the side of the mountain, her tail twitching back and forth. As the gravel shot out from beneath the great cat's feet, I gave a silent prayer of thanks for her visit. I knew it was a sign. I had asked for one while I was writing, and it came unexpectedly. I had brought with me to the desert the *Medicine Cards* by Jaime Sams and David Carson, a type of animal divination when used intuitively helps the person gain deeper insights into a situation. I've used these cards throughout my life and always seem to travel with them. Sprinting back to my room, I pulled the deck out and searched for mountain lion. I scanned the information:

"The balance of body, mind, and spirit."

When we honor our intuition, we awaken a part of ourselves that has always existed in balance with our body, mind, and spirit. It is up to us to be aware of our own natural guidance, the intuition, which empowers each of us to live a richer more meaningful life:

Watch for the signs.
Open your heart.
Listen to your intuition.

CHAPTER TWO

Revealing or Concealing:
Fear of Being Stigmatized

~~

Like many children my parents told me my intuition
was my imagination. I felt different, less than, like I didn't
fit in and there was something wrong with me.
I was made to feel that I didn't fit in.
Cher Lyn

The twelve people I interviewed for this book are working or middle class women with varying upbringings and professions. I interviewed an animal communicator; a professor, an astrologer, a scientist/artist, a shamanic artist, a college student, a physical therapist, a nurse, a theater director, a self taught anthropologist, a real estate agent, and a business owner. About half of the women I interviewed feel stigmatized for their intuitive abilities. They make a conscious decision not to share their certain intuitive aspects with some people. They prefer to keep their intuitive abilities "hidden" so as not to break with societal expectations associated with being a woman, a mother, or a professional. But these same women routinely claim their "insights," as the term "insight" carries an acceptable connotation in society. To have *insight* into a specific event, or *insight* into how another person is feeling, is usually deemed socially acceptable.

What exactly is the relationship between a woman's intuition and her identity, and why do some choose to conceal this part of their identity? The stigma placed upon them by society for being intuitive can lead to shame and fear. And yet, the women in this book talk about their worth when using intuition as a source of inspiration, and a tool for daily guidance. One of the women I interviewed, Claire, made the conscious decision to reveal her intuitive gifts to the world. She knew and acknowledged her intuition from a very early age.

Claire is a well-known astrologer with a Master's degree in Psychology. She is only 5 foot 3, but she has a solid presentation of self and I sensed her old soul wisdom as she began talking. She is confident, funny, and easily laughs at her self. As soon as we began speaking I felt humbled by Clair's confidence in her intuitive gifts:

I was born pretty much with my spiritual nature intact. And, I was always very different from every one around me. It never occurred to me to buy into anyone else's system. I was just always different from birth on.

When I asked if she recognized in her teenage years that she was different from her friends, or if she had a knowing that she was unusual, her comment to me was even more startling:

I am so self-referenced. Some people think about what other people think, but I've always thought what other people think is none of my business. And, I've always had guides if you will, so I recognized I was different. It has never been an issue. I just am who I am.

Claire's strong sense of self was refreshing. She does not appear to have the vacillations that many of us go through as we attempt to find our place in the world.

Claire reveals her intuitive gifts to the larger public mainly because she doesn't care what they think. It was not so easy for me. I have worried that people will judge me poorly if they find out that people's guides and angels speak through me.

Sarah, one of the women I interviewed concealed her intuitive gifts from her father because she feared he would think she was crazy. Sarah is the youngest of the women I spoke with, in her early twenties. She began seeing, with her peripheral vision, dead family members and strangers when she was 4-years-old. Tall, athletic, and energetic, with an open face and lovely clear eyes, we agreed to discuss her expereinces with her intuition. We met at my house, a quiet Saturday morning before Thanksgiving.

After her grandmother's death when she was four, Sarah began drawing angels on the margins of her pictures she drew and painted. Her mother routintely asked, "Who is that?" She always replied, "Grandma." During family dinners she remembers:

> *I don't think I have ever really physically seen a whole*
> *person, it's not like the movies, you know when you see*
> *the whole being. It's in my peripheral vision. When I was*
> *a kid, my stepdad would sit at the head of the table, my*
> *mom across from me, I would look over at my mom and*
> *I could see behind her the outline of my Grandma, and*
> *I would tell her, "Grandma is here, Mom." My mom, I*
> *think, was really scared of it at first, and so she kind of*
> *ignored it, so I really didn't develop it, and it shut off.*

Sarah's mother began to develop her own intuition a few years later and took Sarah to a psychic. The psychic asked Sarah if she saw anybody in the room, and Sarah immediately saw her grandmother:

> *I remember seeing really bright lights in the corner and*
> *[the psychic] helped me to acknowledge it by confirming*
> *that she had seen her sitting in the corner too.*

Sarah's mother took her to other psychics over the course of several years. Her intuitive abilities opened up further allowing her to "see" more deceased people. But it began to take a toll. Spirits began to talk to her all the time—at home, school, and while she was trying to do work:

> *They would bother me all the time. It takes a lot of ener-*
> *gy out of you. I couldn't do my work and I couldn't sleep*

*at night. I would tell my mom there were too many peo-
ple walking around my room [laughter]. It's taken more
years to accept this, but during middle school when I
was 12 to 14-years-old was when I really embraced it
and then learned how to shut it off.*

Her middle and high school years were unusual by all ac-
counts with her visionary and auditory awareness of the dead
people. She could hear and see spirits everywhere:

*I remember sitting in class in middle school and I would
see spirits walking through the doors—I guess doorways
are entry points for spirits walking through ... I would
just see constant figures walking in and out and it was
distracting to me. The spirits were just moving around. I
couldn't really hear them all. I have to be really focused
to hear them.*

Sarah does not disclose these abilities to friends for fear of being
judged. For now, she prefers to quietly keep her intuitive talents
to herself:

*I think it's because I don't feel confident enough. I'm not
ready. I feel weird. I don't want to be judged or come
across as the wrong person. Besides that, it was hard.
I need to figure things out in my own life. I need to be
more established.*

Renee, an artist and scientist raised with a strong Catholic
upbringing hid her childhood intuition because she was afraid

of being ostracized by her family. She is passionate and vibrant, small in stature, with an easy laugh and warmth that drew me to her immediately. Her clothes are bright, the color of oceans and sunsets. She wears dangling earrings, and a long necklace of dolphins and crystals. We sat at the kitchen table drinking tea with my dog, Preston, who sat at Renee's feet. She has led an extraordinary life filled with world travel, children, marriages, divorces, and self awakenings.

Born in Canada, Renee's family moved to the United States, then, soon after, to Brazil, where she was raised. She has a bachelors degree in visual communication and art, and speaks Portuguese and English fluently. Catholicisim was integral to her upbringing, while studying in Catholic schools shaped her early beliefs in the world and people around her:

I'm very grateful for my Catholic roots. My connection to Christ, the Mother Mary, the Saints—there was a lot of good in it. What really kicked my butt was fear based— Heaven and Hell—the devil, sin, guilt that comes with that belief system that we really don't need.

In her first marriage due to her Catholic upbringing she felt haunted with intense guilt, sin, and fear. As a grown woman with two small children living in Brazil, she questioned her intuition which appeared in the form of premonitions. Her husband at that time would not allow her to work outside the home. One day Renee had a nervous breakdown. Her family admitted her to a psychiatric clinic for a week. When she went home, her marriage began to unravel and she became depressed. She eventually sought a divorce, and the divorce became her milestone for gaining self awareness. Renee learned through a painful growth process that to hide who she was and to disavow her passions and gifts leads to great unhappiness:

> *I don't know what really happened to me. I just let go— who I was what the world was about. I just lost contact with this reality. It was really scary. I needed intervention. One of the things I always had was, "I am an intelligent person. I have a brilliant mind." Then all of a sudden I lose my mind. It threw me back into a bad space. I wanted to fit in with the world, but in order to fit in I was untruthful to myself.*

After the divorce, Renee found the courage to move in a new direction. She knew that there was more to life than what Catholicism had taught her, and she began meeting new people. One of these people was a medium who did healings inside her home. She would channel a guide who was an Amazon Indian. Renee moved deep out of her comfort zone, but loved the stimulation and new information that framed her reality. She discovered she hadn't lost her mind, but on an unconscious level was fearful of her world collapsing. Once she opened herself up to the idea that a new way of thinking about the world and how she could interact in it, she felt acceptance and peace with herself:

> *I was 28, and started my spiritual quest to really under-*

stand what this world is about and who I am. I met with a journalist. He took me to a priest who measured peoples auras with a machine. Then I traveled to a city called São Lourenço, to interview an astrologer and numerologer who became a teacher of mine.

Renee's life shifted with her spiritual quest. After learning Cabalistic numerology and some astrology, she began working with crystals in nature for healing the earth. She was introduced to a type of healing work in nature called Geobiology. Geobiology works with rebalancing the earth's energies with the use of quantum tools, sacred geometry, sound frequencies and musical instruments like drums and Tibetan bowls. This techique is also known as land clearings and house clearings that restore the earth's health by healing the influences of everything from electric to electronic, and geopathic stress. She works much like being an urban shaman clearing pollution from the air and the environment using techniques that bridge science and spirituality. She has many spiritual helpers like angels and nature spirits to do these clearings:

In order to do this work you need to work co-creatively with nature and acknowledge that everything is alive, everything has consciousness.

Renee became well known in Brazil for her work and conducted in the course of a few years over dozens of land clearings that she did as gifts. Then, with a further shift into her own abilities and comfort with her skills, Renee began charging for her services and teaching Geobiology around the world:

I set up a mandala with my tools and essences. I tell people I'll be doing a ceremony in their space, home, or the place where they want the clearing performed at. I explain that the sacred soils and waters from different parts of the world hold energy. I use essential oils to balance the physical, emotional, and mental bodies of the home. When I offer the essences, our energy fields are intertwined with the land and the home creating harmony and balance all around us. Whatever happens to the person, happens to the home and vice versa. The impact of a clearing when the owner participates opens their consciousness to interacting in a new way with nature and the environment. Their home is an extension of themselves. After the clearing, there is always a noticable positive shift in the energy of the house and of the people who inhabit the location enhancing their health and awareness. I get to witness profound human and environmental transformation.

For Renee, the cost of not acknowleging her intuition led to depression, a bottoming out, and then as she picked up the pieces of her life, she experienced a self transformation that allowed her intuition to shine out. The transformation that she witnessed in her clients was a mirror back to her for her own transformation. When we put a stake in the ground, and are willing to own the pieces that are a part of us that have been deemed unworthy by others or ourselves, we take root in ourselves in new and unimaginable ways.

The women interviewed for the book have all to some extent experienced a self transformation. Renee overcame her stigma of revealing her intuitive information to people, and as a result, has helped countless people around the world with her Geobiology work. Sarah, feels stigmatized with her intuitive abilities to see and hear the dead. She wants to overcome this feeling, growing more into her talents to shine out confidently in the world. Claire was born knowing she was different, and because of that, didn't care what others thought about her. Her self transformation was the awakening into astrology that sustains and supports her on a daily basis. Each women's self transformation is unique, and an opening to a wider expansive part of themselves.

We always have choices in our lives. It is up to you to take the chance, to take the first step in every new situation. When you belive in yourself and do what you love, the opportunity for self-growth and transformation become the everyday experience and not the exception to the rule. Sarah, Renee, and Claire each came from a different viewpoint in life with their intuition. Sarah, while still growing into a deeper degree of comfort with her intuition, allowed the spirits to talk to her. Renee, left one way of life that was unhappy and stifling to her, into a completely new paradigm of life that wholly supported her awakening into a gifted Geobiologist. Claire, knew from the earliest age that she was different—and celebrates this difference as a way of life. Claire's words have stayed with me:

> *You know, just trust your gut always. Listen to your dreams. Spend a lot of time alone. Truth was always my survival mechanisim.*

CHAPTER THREE

Alexis—The "Silent Intuitive"

~~

*I view myself as a "Silent Intuitive" because things just
happen and I smile to myself, and say, "Thank you for helping,
thank you for helping this person." I look at everybody that I
end up treating with physical therapy as someone very special.*

Alexis

Alexis was raised in Massachusetts. She is a soft-spoken woman in her early fifties with hazel eyes. She is dressed fashionably in leather boots, jeans, and a long cream sweater. Alexis has a strong nurturing presence that comes, in part, from a life of caretaking. A physical therapist, she works with the elderly to help them maintain their physical coordination and mobility. She also laughs easily and her expression is compassionate and direct. Alexis has one child, Sarah, who was also interviewed for this book. Her second husband, Paul, Sarah's stepfather, was diagnosed with late stages Alzheimer's disease at 62-years-old. The initial stages of Alzheimer's for Paul left gaps in his memory that steadily worsened. He is also a Vietnam vet who was exposed during the Vietnam War to Agent Orange. He has suffered other debilitating health consequences as a result of his exposure. At first, Alexis mentions, they were small things like the front door being left open for hours as he watched television or listened to the radio. Then, the faucet water in the bathroom was left on while she left the house to do errands. At another time, while driving, Paul began forgetting where he was going, and would call her for directions to the local grocery store. His driving privileges were revoked, and Alexis maintained the care of their home, and all of life's daily necessities, monitoring him closely. Paul is also a highly skilled wood craftsman, and after an incident with power tools, they needed to be removed and the next stage of care evaluated. Paul was recently admitted to a care facility for advanced stages of Alzheimer's and dementia. Alexis looks at the road ahead of her now one day at a time. Her bravery in the face of this loss on so many levels is a remarkable feat.

As we moved into the discussion of her intuition, she recounted many instances of "knowing" aspects of Paul's condition, and having him evaluated initially to get the highest quality medical help. There were times when she knew to come early from work or errands to stop a potential catastrophe from happening. For the past four years, Alexis has battled the healthcare system to get the best possible resources for her husband. She has maintained a steady positive nature while supporting her husband and working full-time helping others battle their physical difficulties.

Alexis's hands are an important aspect of the intuitive work she does with her physical therapy patients. Her hands tingle when she places them over patients' injuries and the patients report that her hands feel hot:

There are a lot of times my hands will just do something and I don't think about it. I feel divinely guided. I hate writing patient notes because everything has to be documented so thoroughly and sometimes I may not have the rationale for doing what I do.

Alexis uses her intuition to guide her hands in the healing of her patients. She does not need to look at any medical charts to diagnose the location of their pain, rather she closes her eyes, and allows her intuition to guide her hands where they are needed most on the patient's body. Alexis keeps her intuitive work to herself. Her patients increased mobility and healing are satisfaction in and of itself for Alexis. She recounts one story of a patient:

A coworker gave me a patient she couldn't see that day because she had to leave early. The patient had had a stroke with a one-sided weakness, in a lot of pain, upset, and didn't want to participate in therapy. I worked with her that day, she was very pleasant, not complaining at all. The next day her therapist asked me what I did. The patient the next day was able to get out of bed on her own and walk to a chair without any pain. Her therapist said it was a miracle—this lady, all of a sudden, was like a different person.

This story is not unusual for Alexis. She sees herself as a conduit for the divine healing that comes from her hands and is given to those in her care.

Alexis's mother was a significant role model despite being a strict parent. Even-keeled, surrounded by friends, and full of positive energy, Alexis' mother was demonstrative with her love and always wanted the best for Alexis. Alexis' ideological upbringing was strictly Catholic: she experienced few if any intuitive insights as a child. After she moved away from home, in her twenties, she broke away from Catholicism and began exploring astrology. Alexis explains:

Well, I'm a medical person. Astrology is science-based, with all of the planets and coordinates. It is an exact science that can be done with a computer. People don't have to do it by hand anymore. It is more concrete—as opposed to someone who calls herself a psychic.

Alexis focused her attention on astrology and physical therapy throughout her thirties and forties. She was aware that her intuitive nature was growing during this period. She began seeing bright patterned lights and she could feel the presence of people, or souls, though she could see no one. Alexis explained that she has always been curious about numbers and money, and she realized she could use her keen intuition for the practical purpose of investing in the stock market. She asked for help from the universe and not long after Alexis began trading in the market a spirit named "Amble" began visiting her, giving her good advice on the market. At first she could just feel his presence in the room, but later he began speaking to her:

> *Amble would help me with my trading by turning the computer off, or by not letting me get on to my computer. I had several instances where I couldn't get the trade through, and then he helped me. My daughter drew a picture of Amble. He is short, balding man with a pinstripe bottom and top, holding an umbrella with dollar signs dropping instead of rain on the paper. He stayed for a while but then he left. Amble made me laugh, he was so unpredictable, seemed to love being here and helping me play the stock market.*

Alexis often channels her intuitive gifts using a divination system called "Destiny Cards." With a regular deck of cards Alexis uses a system based on birth cards and primary ruling cards. Clients seek out Alexis to glean information about major life events such as getting married, buying a house, or starting a new business. She explains that she uses her intuition in the reading of the card spread, but the information is not set in stone. Alexis sees herself as the conduit for the cards:

> *I am teaching you how to fish; I'm not giving you the fish. You need to make it relevant. Some people just*

want to know this is going to happen or that is going to happen. I see it as giving people information to help them, and as time goes on the information will work out the way it should. I've learned to be more quiet and discerning. I also believe I became more confident. When you're learning something you need to prove something, but now there's no need to prove anything after all these years. I don't get up in the morning and say to myself, "Oh, I think I'm going to be intuitive today. It's a very natural way of life. I like to help people. To give to people the best I can do for them."

As Alexis accepted herself more and more, her intuitive gifts grew which have helped her life to blossom. Alexis explained that her intuitive practice even helped her connect with her beloved dog, Georgia. Alexis' first golden retriever developed an autoimmune deficiency disease, then an infection, and died overnight at fifteen months old. Alexis was heartbroken and decided to manifest a good, healthy female dog who would be named Georgia. Over the course of a few months, Alexis grew frustrated because there seemed to be only male puppies available. She spoke to an intuitive who said that there was a female litter of Goldens that would soon appear and to just be patient. The next day Alexis discovered a new listing for an all-female litter of Golden Retrievers. Alexis remembers visiting the golden puppies that very day:

We visited the woman's home, she was so sweet. She had a son who was also there helping with the dogs and he was handicapped. He told me the dogs would do well in the hospital as service dogs. I always wanted to work with a dog in the hospital to help people in recovery. I looked at the dogs, they all had ribbons around their necks; I love purple, so I picked the dog with the purple ribbon, and the woman said, "Why, that's our little Georgia."

Naturally, Alexis chose Georgia and has trained her to work with elder care patients in hospitals. She says Georgia was born to this work, and the training was easy for them both. They are an inseparable pair, and Georgia has supported Alexis throughout her ordeal with Paul's illness.

Alexis views herself as an "energy sensor," and she feels her daughter Sarah, is a visionary, who has her own intuitive sense:

Sarah has seen my husband's mother, a lady with red hair who died before she was born. My husband's father died when she was nine. He was driving a truck, lost control and hopped a median. After a month in the hospital he died. Sarah described his accident to a tee, including his jacket and pocket watch. She always drew pictures, and there was always in angel in the corner, a bright, bright, light that was my mother.

Sarah described encounters with a playmate who had died, but visited her and helped throughout her childhood:

As a kid I used to tell my Mom I had an imaginary friend, Mr. Congoats. I think he was a Civil War soldier

*that came back—he was always holding a gun or a stick,
he was an older man. I used to tell Mom, "I'm going to go
play with Mr. Congoats." He just talked to me. We would
hang out. He was just there when I was a kid, five or six.*

Sarah also communicated with a classmate who committed
suicide. According to Alexis, the classmate was unable to leave
his home without speaking to his dad and telling him how sorry
he was—he wanted to be forgiven for what he did. The boy's
spirit began to visit Sarah in her bedroom. Sarah was fourteen
at the time. Alexis remembers how:

*Sarah would physically see him sitting at the end of her
bed. He started to bother her way too much. I let her talk
to an intuitive about him, and she said that Sarah needed to address this issue and he would go away. I brought
her to the neighbor, the father, and he was not very
open-minded. He challenged her, but she handled him
very matter-of-factly and told him, "Your son is sorry
for what he did, he would like for you to forgive him,
and if he had to do it over again he would have faced
his life rather than taking his own life." And that was
that. He never bothered my daughter again. Sarah was
very brave, and that was the first time she ever talked to
anyone outside the family about her intuitive abilities.*

The experience helped Alexis understand that it was critical
to teach Sarah *discernment*. Discernment can be tricky business
when you are dealing with those you cannot see in the physi-

cal realm. But coping with the spirit world is like everyday life, there must be proper boundaries and respect.

If a friend or stranger is bothering you—you let them know it's not okay. The same holds for the souls who may visit, if you have this particular type of intuition. If the visitation is too much and interferes with your life in an unhealthy way, or does not feel good to you—then put up your boundary and say, "Go away!" In Sarah's case she made the decision to help and give the father the information, but that decision may not be for everyone. You are within your own rights here to say, "No," and move on with your life. Pay attention to how you feel and what makes you comfortable. Careful boundaries will help you maintain a healthy balance between rationality and intuition.

Alexis uses her hands in deep connection with others during physical therapy work. She doesn't question the energy she feels flowing through her to help another. As an "energy sensor," she puts herself in the line of fire every day to use her hands with clients who struggle with the daily functionalities of life. Because of her deep trust with her intuition, Alexis has grown into a place in life that is in harmony and peace. Every interaction she encounters with other people in her job is a connection to the healing power available to each of us.

The ability to unhook from the reality around us and tap into that inner reservoir of knowing that is our individual compass requires trust and faith. To have faith in our own unique selves is the ability to trust in the path before us. Even if that path is not meticulously laid out with each juncture clearly marked. A powerful reminder from Claire is the idea of being "self-referenced" which negates the idea of believing in anything that society has to say about your own life as a truth. A key, according to Claire, is the trust she has gained in the belief of her own gifts:

> *I was always a truth teller, and I knew I always saw truth. I wouldn't have said as a kid, "I'm here to tell people what the truth was" because I didn't reference anything in terms of other people. But I always knew I saw truth. In regards to a career, I knew I wanted to work with horses, and so I worked with horses. Then, I was attracted to astrology and I did that.*

Talking to Alexis has shown me again, that using one's intuition is an expression of self that grows more and more as we allow ourselves to *trust* and give to others. There is no formula to having trust. There is no ritual to acquiring trust. People try to complicate things too much like thinking there is a right way to do things. It's really all about spending enough time with ourselves to find what our truth is about. It's as simple as that. Using that "gut" feeling can open up a world of possibilities waiting to happen.

Alexis demonstrates that intuition is a natural function of who she is and allows it to guide her on a daily basis. She doesn't have to think about using intuition—it's always there. When we use intuition as a natural expression of ourselves, it guides us into situations that we may have not had access to if we weren't paying attention. Alexis used her intuition to guide her with her husband Paul; with patients at her job; and her daughter Sarah's difficult disclosure of her abilities to a neighbor. In each instance, her life choices were spot on because she was confident in her abilities to trust, and then follow on the internal advice she received from her intuition. Alexis says:

Every single part of our life is a puzzle that fits together, and yes, we can question it, but this is where you are supposed to be right now, at this minute. It doesn't mean we are not going to move on and do other things, not to negate the present, because this is a bridge to the other side. I think people are so busy, and don't sit and allow themselves to think about where they're at, and be in the present knowing this is where they are supposed to be. I allow myself to be present and let the energy flow naturally.

When you follow your intuition, you can help others as well as yourself. Your body becomes a conduit for the divine healing energies to come through and assist others. Because Alexis lives with the awareness of her intuitive capabilities, she lives in the moment with joy, and a knowing of her place in the world. Her daughter, Sarah, is growing more and more into her intuitive gifts and helping others.

CHAPTER FOUR

Cher Lyn—Shamanic Visionary Art

~~

I came from an abusive childhood. In my twenties,
I tried to kill myself and continued to want to die for a year.
I realized after a time the Angels weren't going to let me die.
It became obvious that I was meant to
live. So, I decided to do life.
Cher Lyn

I had met Cher when I was giving a workshop on channeling. She was sitting across the room on a large blue pillow staring at me intently. She's 5'9" tall, long limbed, with blond hair hanging straight below her shoulders. Her light green eyes radiate intensity. Cher was a photo and TV commercial model who worked in fashion houses throughout the world. She was entirely focused on me during the workshop, nodding her head in agreement. After the workshop was over, Cher walked over to me and pointedly asked me who I was and where I had been.

She told me she was an artist and was only in town to deliver a painting to a client. She had seen my brochure for the workshop in a store window after dropping the painting off, and came to the event because she was intuitively nudged.

Cher is an extraordinary oil and acrylic painter, a visionary artist and mystic, who paints breath-taking life size shamanic goddesses and scenes of nature and animals on huge canvases. Her paintings reflect the spiritual, and a deep love of nature and animals. She adds small pieces of nature she finds on walks—sticks, stones, crystals and even buffalo hair to the paintings. Since I first met her, I have visited Cher in several places she calls home, and in each domestic space, there is a powerful natural element that is representative of her extremely dynamic inner life.

The first home of Cher's I visited was a brick colored two-bedroom log cabin. It was nestled on the creek side of slow moving water, on about an acre of green land, with large cottonwood trees lining the water's edge. A giant California oak tree with foot thick gnarled branches swept the side of the cabin, and an oval red wooden deck was built around this magnificent oak tree. The tree was absolutely massive, and was probably 300 years or more old. I walked in her cabin front door, and immediately noticed the large stone fireplace that dominated the room. A four-foot by five-foot painting in cobalt blue of a bare-breasted goddess rested on the mantle. The wooden floors were covered with scattered sheepskin rugs, wooden candlesticks of all sizes were in every nook and cranny of the room, as well as a variety of crystals, seashells, and two large conch shells.

Knee high bronze statues of Quan Yin stood in different corners of the room flanked by baskets of peacock feathers. The space paid an aesthetic and loving tribute to the natural world.

As I would soon learn, Cher has an intensely intuitive relationship with nature that she has been able to express through her art and her daily life:

> *I have this deal with Creator, show me the magic and I'll stay. The more I did ceremony and honored the earth and nature and sat in gratitude, the more I felt at home and comfortable and saw more magic. Then I saw the magic come through my paintings.*

She stood up after she said this and showed me the rest of the cabin, a large bedroom on the bottom floor, a small room filled with all of her paints and jars of brushes, a tiny kitchen, and a loft upstairs. We climbed up a wooden kiva ladder to access the loft and there were more sheepskin rugs, a small couch, and a meditation area with an altar. Her altar was filled with artifacts of nature such as wood, shells, and various crystals. The smell of incense filled the space of this special place, and there was a deep feeling of peacefulness.

Cher's parents were church minded, and Cher and her brother always went to Sunday school. But Cher's childhood was emotionally and spiritually devastating:

> *I ran away from home when I was fifteen. I came from an abusive childhood—sexually abused from my father and grandfather. I spent years having a strong sense of*

intuition but not understanding what it was. Like many children, my parents told me it was my imagination. … Since I was a child I could see the future—I had premonitions, dreams, knowings, and so many visions. I've had very exact, prolific dreams. In one, I saw myself holding a bird and the bird flies away. Then my son wakes me up and says, "There's a bird outside." I go outside to pick up a bird in my hand and it flies away.

While we did not explore Cher's childhood, she did explain that when she ran away from home, she went to an uncle's house. She was welcomed by him and he cared for her. He was an artist and became a healthy father figure for a while. One day she climbed a tree that overlooked the ocean, and made a decision that altered the course of her life. She said aloud to the sky and all of nature that she would become a painter. As her art career evolved, her paintings revealed a profound mysticism. Originally her uncle was very supportive of her. But when she began to outpace him he asked her, "Who is this mystic? What is this art?" Eventually he stopped talking to Cher because he thought what she was doing was devil's work.

Cher was devastated:

I didn't want to be here anymore. I wanted to take my life, but the angels wouldn't let me. When I tried, I had the strongest sense that leaving my body wasn't going to work. I knew that I would just have to come back again and live another life all over again. When I was twenty-five I had my second son and began painting every

day. I tapped into my passion, and that gave me reason
for being here.

The loss of her uncle only helped to strengthen Cher. She gave up worrying about how others judged her work and she focused more on her inner life and the creation of her "Soul Paintings." People from all walks of life have contacted Cher to create soul paintings for them. She uses her intuition to "paint" the soul of the person. I watched her start a soul painting and felt the space we were sitting in become electrically charged. There were jars and jars of paint brushes; abalone shells filled with incense; crystals; her medicine rattle; bird feathers; a drum with sacred symbols painted on it; shells, sticks, and stones; and sacred, blessed water. Cher sat cross-legged on the ground and said:

The soul paintings bring through the higher aspect of self.
I make a prayer, an invocation. I don't even have to meet
the person, but will make contact over the phone with
them. I invite their higher selves to work with my high-
er self. I also ask that anything that needs to be shown
to me, I see. I bless the canvas with sacred water, grid-
ding it with crystals and sacred geometry. I say prayers
before I lay any paint on the canvas. Once I put paint
on the canvas, I get hit with the colors needed. I add
essences of the earth, but it's different with each person
and painting. After the paint dries, I spend a lot of time
meditating with the painting and waiting until Spirit
has something to show me. I see the images in my mind

of what I'm meant to paint. I see it three dimensionally on the canvas. I see it in 3-D, the paint is moving on the canvas, I see images in the paint as it dries.

Cher sometimes plays the didgeridoo over the canvas. Her didgeridoo is five-feet long and made entirely out of hand-spun glass. She sings beautifully and may chant over the painting as well. The intense concentration I witnessed seems to remove her from this world and place her in another. Cher lives, breathes, and walks inside of her intuition every day. She is a glowing reminder that if we follow our path and listen to our inner voice, our potential for creativity and happiness is unlimited. But, her journey to use her innate boundless creativity has not been an easy road. She has felt stigmatized throughout her life for making the conscious decision to follow her own path:

I wasn't honored or respected for my work. Actually, I was suppressed from my intuition when I was younger. We all have experiences of giving over our power because we love another. And, we think if we make ourselves smaller we can get along. It's been layers upon layers of unpeeling those pieces of shame. "I don't fit in, I'm wrong, something's not right about me." It's been a lifetime process of realizing those words are not true at all. My identity has been affected positively, I have more fire, more of me shining through, I'm stronger.

Cher exemplifies a true warrior goddess. She is a woman who has walked through the fire of her own life and stands tall in her goddess shoes. Cher's passion for her art, her own inner fire, has fueled a life of intense creativity. Despite judgments against her art, she found her true calling and with true grit, stayed the course. Cher is a guiding light for other women who fear that their own creativity and intuition may be judged. To avoid such judgment, many women make themselves smaller, hiding their unique abilities. In charge of her own destiny, Cher's ability to become a living, breathing vessel of creativity is a powerful example for all of us. She has found her place in the world by calling forth, rather than suppressing, her creativity and intuition.

Cher's art is also a strong reminder that when we honor who we are, we can bring forth dynamic creations to share with the world. In facing the judgments from family and the world, Cher conquered the need for any outside approval, and lives an authentic life, guided steadfastly by her intuition. She says in parting:

> *Trust your heart. The more you sit in your heart,*
> *the more connected to your heart you become.*
> *If I trust, I feel better. Let your heart lead you.*

CHAPTER FIVE

Maia—Healing in Communication with Animals

~~

We're kind of alone a lot of times and no one gets who we are.
I would have these intuitions about things and the world
wasn't a place where I thought I could share them.
Maia Kincaid, Ph.D.

Maia, an animal communicator, hid her intuition from an early age. I met Maia at her home on a cold, stark February afternoon. Maia is medium height, slender, and radiates self-confidence. She wears her shoulder length brown hair tucked behind her ears. The day I interviewed her, she was dressed casually in blue jeans and a white shirt. When I walked inside her home she gave me a hug and told me she was glad that I wanted to listen to her story. But, as I would quickly learn, that self-confidence I first observed did not come easily.

Maia's gift of communciation with animals evolved from her position as a medical intuitive. Her communication with animals manifests in various forms, but usually it is as voices she can hear or pictures she can see. Each animal is different and has its own personality. Almost all of Maia's work is done over the phone and through email. She has clients from all over the world, and recently worked with a Buddhist monastery in Japan with a dog saying to her:

A lot of the animals will lead the humans to me. The humans will say I don't really know why I'm calling you but …

She prefers to transcribe the dialogue she has with the animals, so she can forward the transcription to the owners. One dog explained to Maia that he had, "led his owner to me because the communication was not just for them, but for all of the world." Maia believes that she is driven to do work with animals in order to help both animals and people feel empowered. For example she remembers one dog she communicated with:

He told me the owner needed to do painting. That the owner had been dreaming of painting for twenty years and it was time to start. Then the owner laughed and called his dog a tattletale.

Maia explained that when she was a child she kept her intuitive gifts to herself:

I knew I was different. I think a lot of human beings have that sense. I had intuitions, but it was like there wasn't a place for them to land. A lot of different things were compartmentalized like my relationships, my boy-

friends. I would keep my spirituality and things I knew intuitively to myself. I wouldn't share that part of my life. It was like I would put my intuition into a box. I shut it all down.

Shuting down her intuition evolved from her growing up in an inauthentic spiritual life fostered from a patriarchical style religion. Maia spoke rapidly to me, her hands devoid of any jewlery, moving around the air, completely engrossed in her earlier life:

My parents took us to church, it wasn't real, not full of integrity. Something about the way my parents were participating wasn't authentic. But, I didn't know exactly what it was. Something inauthentic. Something not right.

She felt a dissonance with religion that was compounded by the way her parents participated in the event, playing a part of what society expected of them, but it did not ring truth for Maia. Perhaps due to this, her intuition got muddied when she grew older, due to a social structure that told her what was right and wrong.

After she had started her animal communication business, she had a hard time admitting what she did for work to other people:

When people would ask me what I did in my work I would get this sinking feeling, oh here we go, how do I explain it—then I would get this discomfort. Over the years it began to change.

Part of her intuitive compartmentalization would cause a desire to be needed and feel important, after she had put her intution in a box. This would evolve negatively later in life as she ran her business.

That feeling of wanting to be needed never went away. As an adult, and launching her own business, that "need to be needed" played out in the form of clients, not her usual ones, who would ask for emergency help for their animals. These phone calls would occur inconviently after work hours and throughout the weekends when she was trying to do other things and take a break from her daily responsibilities:

I would take these emergency calls in the evenings, on weekends, going out of town. Not a normal client, someone who would find me in desperation. They found me through the website. It was never satisfying. I'll take this work, like someone who had lost a pet, and there was this urgent thing—I wondered why I kept taking the jobs?

She sought for deeper understanding of the motivations behind her behavior to respond to the phone callers who "needed" her continually after work hours disrupting her privacy with her family and friends. It was a powerful self-realization because it showed a blind spot in her work. As a result, the emergency calls for help completely stopped:

I had this desire to be needed and important, they wanted to be needed. It was like I was the receptor, we fit together. But I was no longer the receptor. Something shifted in me, so I wasn't getting the same results. You're operating in a whole new way. A lot of times we make choices as a kid that stick with us, and we need to learn how to make different choices.

Maia was operating from a childhood pattern of wanting to be needed and desired at all costs. It took the life lesson of constantly responding to people at inappropriate times and not feeling appreciated to help her understand that the pattern of behavior to be "desired and needed" was not important to her any more. She had outgrown a pattern of behavior that was instilled from an early age to change into a healthier way of living and working with her skills.

Maia, like many of the women interviewed in the book, also worked with an outdated belief that her skills and time did not deserve adequate compensation, or any compensation at all. She didn't feel comfortable asking for money for her services. She comforted and gave sage advice on a regular basis to clients about their animals, but when it came to getting paid for her work she explained:

I'm working and intuitively I can help them. Then when the money issue came up, here comes this sinking feeling. I had love for what I was doing, but the financial part was uncomfortable. I would take money and not process it right away. It would sit around. People would send me

*an email and ask me how much and I would never send
them a bill. I didn't think I deserved it.*

There was the issue of self-worth for Maia. The acknowledgement of her service to others as *valuable* was the missing link. There was also elements of self-sabatoge, "I can take just enough money to live off of, but any more I'm not deserving of" is a ticker tape that runs through the minds of many women. In part this is rooted in the past, as there are few if any financial rewards for domestic labor. Unfortunately the undervaluing of women's work remains prevalent and continues to be a struggle for women to overcome.

Maia's issue with money was also tied to the belief that the world would not accept what she did:

*I would say what I do, and then people would have some
weird response! That's the way it used to happen for me.
It's like, which way do I want to present myself? Some
things started to shift for me when I realized that.*

When she began to accept herself and valued her unique intuitive gifts, she felt a profound shift. When she began to respect her work with animals as a legitimate career, she gained the confidence to charge appropriate fees for her services. Since her shift in perception her relationships and finances have been enhanced:

*I now have a better sense of my own value, what I con-
tribute, and don't have that reaction to money. I've noticed an incredible difference to my finances. I can cele-*

brate, and it is good. I really want to make a difference, and I'm sensitive. When it comes down to receiving, it can be really hard. More self-love. I love to give to people, but I wasn't letting them give back to me.

Maia is not the only women I interviewed that intuitively communicated with animals. The astrologer Claire also had intuitive experiences with animals and nature. As a child, she explained that she could always hear animals and nature speak. Claire's path led her to working with astrology with clients, but she remarked the animals always left a strong impression with her because of their ability to stay in the present with time and not plan for the future or live in the past. Another woman I interviewed, Elena, has telepathic relationship with horses. They send her pictures of what they want or need, as well as words.

I've also had one very powerful animal experience that has stayed with me my entire life. Years ago I went to the fairgrounds to a 4-H show. I had always been drawn to llamas—their inquisitive, intelligent eyes, the bearing of their bodies, and the overall impression that I get from them that they are observing us. The llamas' pen was outside, and a male llama was methodically munching his food. His coat was brown and orange colored, and his eyes were distinct in that I felt they saw everything happening around him. But I made the mistake that because he was an animal in a pen—that he felt inferior and was unhappy with his life. I went up to him staring through the fence, and remember thinking quite clearly as I was watching him, what a shame it was he was in a pen and "owned" by someone, instead of being free in the wild. Just as soon as I finished my thought and was about to walk away, I heard as distinctly as if it was a person standing next to me shouting loudly in my face:

My dear, I am happy to be where I am and serve the humans. It is my role in life to serve and there is no shame in it.

I almost fell over, and the shock on my face made the llama laugh. I was practically sputtering, and said my apologies, and ran away from the pen. The dignity of that llama as he communicated with me showed that we all have a purpose, and to judge another's purpose takes away the dignity of the threads that weave us together.

Because Maia did the work to accept herself she now no longer compartmentalizes her life and she views her intutive gifts as:

A celebration! Like every part of my day is flowing together and not compartmentalized anymore. So now when people come up to me I share what I do with them, they say "It's really interesting, I haven't heard of that before." They have never heard about animal communication, but they want to know about it. There's an excitement about it, because I've changed.

Maia nutured herself, and realized that when she believed in who she was and the value of her contributions, the people around her mirrored back acceptance of her unique gifts that have led to an extraordinary life. For Maia, to communicate with the animal and natural world is as easy and simple as breathing. Maia shares the deep love the animal kingdom has for us and transforms the false belief that we are all separate from each other.

People leave Maia's sessions with a sense of empowerment—knowing that they are loved and that their animals are unconditional in their support. The light that comes from Maia as she talks about the animals and their feelings for us show that by trusting what you feel guided to do for your calling in the world leads to a new awareness of happiness within ourselves. Maia says:

> *It's like the world started to work for me, pulling for me to be my true self, uniquely me. I want to create a world where every human being can hear and communicate with nature and animals.*

CHAPTER SIX

Natalie—Intuition and Teaching

~~

My intuition expanded when I stopped being a people pleaser,
I was able to be more me. When I let that guard down there
was so much richness that was able to come forward.
Natalie

Natalie is a professor who uses her intuitive gifts to help her students. She shows a deep love and caring towards her students. Natalie tells me she trusts her intuition—it has guided and sustained her, and she has witnessed transformations in her students when they are given the tools to become more solid, healthy human beings:

> *I practice my intuitive gifts with my women students. I can sense who is truly unhappy and know who is in a troubled situation. When I am a good listener, and I offer appropriate disclosure of who I am, I find women get empowered and can make different choices for themselves.*

She began our interview recounting when she was twelve years old, and her family was planning to do a house remodel. Her parents intended to send their children to various relatives while the house was being renovated, but she absolutely refused to go—which was completely out of character for her:

> *I was the oldest kid, very compliant. Responsible. I always did what people told me. I stayed home and did odd projects while the remodeling was going on. A friend of ours was doing the remodeling. As it turned out, this man exposed himself to me repeatedly. Was I there because I needed to have this experience? Or was I there to help/protect my mother? There was this intuition not to go to this other relative, but to stay home. I'm still trying to figure it out—the experience was very negative, yet it taught me to trust that sense [the intuition], to be aware!*

Natalie's mother was twelve years old when she was gang raped while picking strawberries in a field. Her mother came from a very large, poor family in a rural part of Ohio. Natalie's mother was the same age as Natalie when the family friend exposed himself to her. Natalie's daughter was molested when she was child but they didn't know it until she was twelve years old. Three generations of women, and none of them knew about the others' sexual abuse until it surfaced when Natalie and her mother were driving to the hospital because her daughter had been hospitalized from an injury:

*My mother and I had a very difficult relationship be-
cause she got divorced. We didn't know why she got
divorced, and then she left the kids behind. We talked
(on the way to the hospital) in the car about trusting,
sexuality, and the power to be a woman first, and then
a mother and wife, instead of losing yourself in those
roles. It was a healing in a sense for us to have a more
communicative relationship.*

Natalie shares these parts of her life with me, eloquently and
with a comfortable directness and compassion. Natalie, who
has a Ph.D. in Education, has short black hair and stylish glass-
es. She wears a colorful array of Native American bracelets that
jingle on her arms. We met in her tiny office that was filled with
vibrant colors, poetry, and photos of her students and grandchildren. Her office felt like a sanctuary, a comfortable space for
a woman who radiated warmth and kindness.

Her intuitive path has been challenging. She has spent the
last decade working with students on an Indian reservation ab-
sorbing their pain. But she has recently learned a listening technique that helps her release it. Natalie folds her hands on her
lap gently, with her hands raised slightly. This small change in
her listening style allowed her to let their pain fall away. There
is almost a Buddha-like presence to Natalie as she describes this
to me. Using this technique, her pain has been transformed to
peace and even more empathy has flowed from her to guiding
her students.

About nine years ago, Natalie's spirituality began to evolve
and change. She was at the end of an unhappy marriage seeking

a divorce and met a man at work. There was an instantaneous connection between them and they became the best of friends. They went on business trips together, chatted for long hours, and enjoyed each other's company. She soon learned that he needed a new kidney to save his life:

> I knew I needed a higher power to help give me the guidance. I was in a very unhappy marriage that was pushing me over the edge to make a decision—I would give a life or lose my life in the process. I was at peace with whatever was going to happen.

She gave her new friend her kidney, and then divorced her husband. She and her friend Stanley became partners. He is Native and she is European. There was resistance from both of their families. But they have a strong connection that outweighs others' judgments. Shortly after they met she visited a Catholic mission with an ancient church, a beautiful, calming spiritual place. She was guided there to call him and describe the location. After she left the mission, there was a bad stretch of a dust clouds on the highway. All of a sudden, she saw in her rearview mirror a large semi truck descending on her. She was penned in on all sides by other cars:

> I said a prayer and closed my eyes. I thought this is why I went to the mission, this is why I had such peace there and then called him. I knew this was my death and I said my goodbyes—the semi barreled down on me. At the last moment the semi rolled off the road. Shaking I real-

ized my phone was ringing—he said, "What happened, what happened?" We are that connected …

After the kidney operation she dreamt there was something going on with Stanley's stomach. She told him to go to the doctor. Sure enough the medical team had left a sponge in his stomach and an infection had formed. He immediately had surgery and he fully recovered, but it was a close call. Natalie saved her partner's life again. Now fully aware of the power of her intuition, it expanded by volumes and she stopped trying to be who others believed she should be. She stopped being afraid to talk about her emotions, and because of this shift, Natalie felt more alive and at peace with her body and self. Natalie opened up to fully trusting her own intuition. In donating a kidney she saved a life, and in the process gained the power to feel confident in her own decision making.

Natalie's courage serves as a reminder that when we believe in ourselves, and the right course of action, our lives serve as a loving connection to others—to help, to heal, and to guide. Strength that we may not even believe we possess comes to the forefront as a natural extension of our talents. With her mother, Natalie healed a pattern of sexual abuse for the women in her family. She guided her daughter into a new place of sovereignty as a woman. For her new partner, Natalie donated one of her own organs to save his life, and in so doing gave his family an opportunity to share precious time together.

Natalie smiles and leaves me with these words:

When I leave this earth I want to know I improved people's lives. So if I can help a man live another eight years to be able to see his child get married, a grandchild—and to know someone believed in them—then I've done my job.

CHAPTER SEVEN

Elena—Trust in Yourself

~~

*I think you have to learn to trust in yourself. I think maybe
if you really sat down, if you really listened, you can remember instances in your childhood where you knew better.
But, you went forward and did that thing anyway and
got into trouble. If you had listened to your intuition
you might have achieved that thing, but taken
a different route to get to that goal.*
Elena

Elena was introduced to me by a friend, Manna, in Colorado.
We were visiting our friends for a Thanksgiving family weekend.
Manna said to me, "I know someone I think you should meet.
She's traveled all over the world, has a connection to Egypt and
has had so many different life experiences." We were leaving on
that Saturday to come back home, but I called Elena and she
was free and open to talking with me. I drove to her house in
the country up a steep driveway, windy and curving up a small
hill. I passed a red barn on my left side. There were no cows or

horses, but when I looked closer I saw six deer sitting around the barn area. Driving a little further up, her house sat on the right. The first thing that struck me was the totem pole embedded in her front door. I've seen totem poles, all kinds—but the door was well over seven feet with a colorful totem pole raising out from the door. It was as if half of the backside of the totem pole was shaved off and then attached to the door. A bird and a bear's face was in the middle of the totem pole. The house structure was log cabin style with large picture windows with views of the surrounding countryside. To the left of the door was a picnic area, a wooden table with a red-checkered tablecloth and old heavy wooden chairs with green vegetation and end of the season flowers in pots.

I knocked on the door and Elena answered with a warm smile crinkling around her light blue eyes. Her silver hair was hanging loosely to her shoulders, and she wore a thick cream colored turtleneck sweater and pants. She invited me into her front room filled with sunlight, and there were colorful hand-woven native rugs hanging on all the walls. She asked me to follow her into the kitchen, and a warm fireplace heated up the area with floor to ceiling windows on one wall. The ceiling was beamed with old wood and hanging from them were handmade baskets of every size and design. Books filled every corner of the room on a host of topics ranging from the philosophical to Shamanic wisdom and an ancient breed of horses—the Akhal-Teke from the Turkmenistan.

I felt so at home in Elena's house. There was a warmth and comfort that invited one to share and speak about the intimacies of life. I began our conversation about the topic of intuition, and if she had any thoughts that came to mind about it:

I think intuition comes from somewhere with God, the Great Spirit, and it's there always to help me. I've always been able to talk and hear what animals were saying. As a kid I was all alone and had a dog, a German Sheppard named Bandito. Bandito liked to tell me jokes. Once I told this raunchy joke and when people asked me where I heard it I told them it was Bandito's joke.

They thought I was a really weird kid! It wasn't until years later that I discovered it wasn't something everyone could do. It was very special. I had telepathy with my dog. When my daughter was born much later, Bandito didn't like it when she had a dirty diaper. He'd pull it off and put it in a corner before I could get to her. When she was learning to walk he'd put himself in front of her and let her grab his fur to help her walk. Before she could walk she would be lying in her basket and Bandito would come over and let her try to grab his tongue. She gained a lot of dexterity with that!

Elena mentioned that her Mom was afraid of dogs and didn't have the same relationship with them that she did, nor did her father. She remembers from an early age that she could talk to not only dogs, but horses, cats, and later, camels. She has an affinity for the whole animal kingdom. With cats, she says they have to get to know you pretty well before they will start talking to you. Elena had a cat named Missy Fouse that spoke to her

one memorable evening after living on her farm for nineteen
years:

> *Look, I'm retiring and I'm going to live with you in your*
> *big barn. I've taken care of your goats for nineteen years*
> *and I think I deserve to be retired and you can feed me.*

Elena said the cat just put the words in her head. She
brought him into the house and bought all kinds of cat food in
tins and bags. But, all he liked were mice—that's all he had eaten
for nineteen years outside. She had to buy mice traps and catch
mice everyday to feed Missy Fouse. If she caught one mouse she
felt lucky. Two mice was a better day, but a three mouse day was
a holiday. She would wiggle the mouse on the floor and he'd eat
them right there. Elena fed her cat that way for two years. Towards the end of the second year she knew he was going to die.
A very special happening let her know that her cat was tran-
sitioning. Missy Fouse was laying on the couch in the sun in
his favorite spot and she was stroking him gently on his back.
Another dog named Shy that had been a part of Elena's life had
recently died. She told her cat that Shy would come and get him
and take him over to the other side. Shy had liked to play soccer with Elena and had a favorite ball that they always kicked
around. The next morning, Missy Fouse died, and the soccer
ball that had been tucked away was right beside the door. Elena
said that was Shy's way of letting her know he had come to get
Missy Fouse. Elena tells me that it's a little far out, but that's the
way her life has always been.

Elena has spent her life as a registered nurse. She was born in Mexico and her family immigrated here to the United States. She wanted to become a vet but her dog Banditio told her to be a nurse! He told her that her first duty was to her own species. Elena has also traveled her entire life throughout the world. She said she was born with a love of traveling—there was a whole world out there with different cultures and different beliefs and that was beautiful. Most of her traveling was with a backpack by herself. On one trip, she was overseas in Jordan at a conference hosted by a US non-profit agency focusing on the environment. In the desert of the Wadi Rum she entered a camel race and won. Her camel's name was Norma. She told me that camels are old wise beings and people don't usually like them, that's why they spit at you. She's toured Iran and Morocco; visited Palestinian refugee camps; went to Turkey with a musician; visited the great pyramids; ridden horses in Egypt; and spent days by herself in Machu Picchu.

I asked her what would you tell women about traveling with her intuition? Elena seems to listen to her own heart and leaves her fears behind. She has such a strong sense of self:

Don't be afraid of anything. Fear is an emotion that I was born without, I'm not afraid of any animal or person. So don't be afraid to approach people you see with love in your heart. Let your heart lead. You're kind of nice and I love you. People take that the wrong way. It's not a sexual love but a spiritual love. And then wherever you go, you'll actually have more fun with yourself, meet more people and have more fun in general. Get a CD and learn some words in the language you're traveling. Carry a dictionary of the language. Be respectful of the customs and the culture of the country.

Elena followed her intuition traveling, and as a result has spent a remarkable life meeting people and talking with them. She also has spent a lifetime talking with the animal kingdom and listening to what they say to her. I asked Elena what wisdom she would share with others about their own intuition:

We are born with intuition but not many believe in it. There is a mind/spirit/physical connection—for women to follow their intuition, to follow their heart and to listen.

CHAPTER EIGHT

Kathryn—Theatre and Performance

~~

Step aside and let go.
Embrace life.
Kathryn

I drove to meet Kathryn at her home in the mountains. As I pulled up into her driveway, I admired a regal oak tree that stood in the front of her yard. A two-foot tall wooden statue of Quan Yin, a Chinese goddess of compassion and unconditional love, sat by her front door amongst herbs and a small, aged wooden bench. I walked over to the tree as I noticed tiny objects around its base, which turned out to be miniature chairs, tables, and small carpets. I smiled to myself. It was so whimsical and sweet, an altar to the fairies. Kathryn opened the door with a smile, quietly giving me a hug. Kathryn has a Ph.D. in theatre and has worked in various fields of performance for almost forty years.

I noticed her dark, cherry wood floors were shiny and clean; each board in the floor looked well cared for. A piano sat in one corner, and by the front window overlooking the tree was a table made from an old door and covered with a purple piece of velvet and beads. She had a piano stool to sit on, and next to the door table, a grouping of plants vibrating with life and health. Kathryn mentioned she had recently taken up beadwork as she pulled out a wicker basket filled with containers of large and small beads, silver and gold beads, large stones and mother of pearl shells. Kathryn's home is as peaceful as are her gardens. Part of the backyard is an herb garden. A garden path of elegant flagstones crisscrosses the backyard, and groupings of chairs with bright cushions sit in garden corners. Kathryn's trees that she planted long ago in her backyard have now grown to maturity. They vibrate with a life force and deep-rooted sense of well-being.

Kathryn has an impish smile that reveals her adventuresome spirit. Kathryn's mother, who is also a painter, lives in a separate home on the back of Kathryn's and her husband Martin's property. Her mother who is in her late 80's recently had a showing at a local gallery of *60* of her most recent landscape watercolor paintings. There is a deep love between Kathryn and her mother, Manna. Kathryn's daughter, Sienna, is a new college student and she shares her mother's and grandmother's passion for creativity, well-being, and integrity. Kathryn's husband, Martin, is a tall, silver-haired charismatic man, a motivational speaker and executive training coach who travels around the world. When he is home, he loves to create new food recipes for his family.

Their home life is easy going and without pretention. Friends stop by frequently and unannounced. Kathryn says:

All your relationships—good ones and bad ones—affect your journey and who you are. What I do impacts and empowers (or disempowers) others around me. My work as a department chair can empower people to do their jobs. We can be leaders in the place where we are right now—empowering people no matter where we are. I think you need to listen to what's going on. Really sense what's happening with the people in your life.

Seated on her deep purple couch with our shoes off, in front of Kathryn's fireplace, we began discussing how she uses her intuition in everyday life. Kathryn is guided by her own creativity and brings to life the creativity of others by crafting original works and performances. Kathryn has used her intuition throughout her career. For example, whenever she is ready to create a performance, the right one at the right time appears:

It just drops on my lap. Every single project has just come to me. I've been doing this for more than thirty years and it just appears. You have to let it talk to you. The thing is realizing it's not me, not my ego, not my creation—it's the piece telling me what I need to know. The hard part is letting the piece tell you what it needs to be. And, it doesn't always come in a timely manner. I read Ann Bogart's book, A Director Prepares, *and she was reflecting back to an incident. The stage performance wasn't working, and she turned to the performers telling them she knew what it needed to be. But, she had no idea. She was hoping that as she walked from the house to the stage, the piece would tell what it needed. In the five seconds of that walk, she got it! I've been in the same situation. It's not really working, I have to say to myself, "I have no idea," and then you have to trust.*

For most of her career, Kathryn believed that her creativity and intuition were guided by her own thought processes, but, eight years-ago she began to ask, "Where does this come from? Where do the answers come from?" Ultimately she realized that she was not listening to her own thoughts; rather the work or piece itself was telling her what she needed to do:

I think there's a moment, an evolution where you have to let go of your own vision and let the piece have its own vision. I'm not in control of this; I am a conduit to let it happen. What does the work need? "Listen, let go," I say that to the students. Is that really what the piece needs? Are you getting in the way of the process? Step aside or zoom out.

Working with the actors on a performance Kathryn understands intuitively how elements of the play need to be, but she feels a need to conceal how she came to her conclusions:

When you're working and it needs to be this way for a performance and then the actors ask you, "Why?" it can't be because I can see this or feel that—it needs to

be, "Well because of the line on the symmetrical." You
need to give them more logical reasons—rational and
scientific way of speaking.

Kathryn has been fighting against the stigma of being a woman in her field and trying to bring a different thought process to the dominant patriarchal environment. She does not feel the need to accommodate the males in her field, but rather works in the collaborative spirit with colleagues—both male and female—who value and also respect her way of thinking and working in the world.

An important shift in Kathryn's life has been the ability to let go:

I've learned to let go of many things. I've learned to
connect my environment with my spiritual landscape.
Making sure my physical environment feeds my home,
and the work environment is empowering and also feeds
my spiritual environment. They reflect each other. Isn't
everything we do mystical? I think there are multiple
levels of things happening all the time. Multiple reali-
ties. Space and time is what humans have created, an
artificial creation that we are in. We forge ahead and do
what we can do.

By allowing our rational minds to step aside to make room for the intuitive process, Kathryn feels and sees things that others do not. It does not mean that others are lacking the ability to "see" the situation as Kathryn does, but rather, they have not yet fully explored and accepted their intuitive abilities. Once a person accepts their ability to use intuition, then they can become the conduit for its expression in the world. For Kathryn, that has evolved into a highly successful theatre career. Kathryn uses her intuition to flow with the ideas in the moment, and then acts definitively from that guidance. Kathryn values both the intuitive and listening skills it requires to guide and empower her students and performers on their own journeys. She hopes to plant these seeds of inner awareness so her students and performers can find the peace to listen for the answers:

Just let go. Embrace life. Let go.

CHAPTER NINE
Franny—Premonitions and Angels

~~

I had flying dreams and visions. I could fly around the room.
That was a big deal to me because I had a fear of heights,
but I kept flying whenever I could.
Franny

I met Franny one sunny, clear blue-sky afternoon while walking around a local art fair. Her booth had been at the fair for many years in the past, but on this particular summer day, I saw her artwork and stopped hard on my heels. On the wall of the booth was a gorgeous work of three Native American women dancing in traditional dress. Holding hands, their expressions were joyous. I was moved by the soulfulness of the painting. I looked around the booth at her other work of horses, burros, sheep, and Native American children. I was struck by the colors and sheer beauty of each subject. The artist seemed to know the people and animals she painted on fabric.

Franny is a batik artist, one of a small group of such artists in the United States. This ancient art form requires artists to use wax and dyes to paint images on cloth. She has been working in this particular medium for forty-two years. On that sunny afternoon, I was drawn to her kindness and goodness immediately, and knew she would be one of the women I interviewed for this book. I loved her gorgeous spirit, and felt a kindred tie to this lovely woman. Franny is in her sixties, slender, about five foot five with short, brown honey colored hair that she tucks behind her ears. At the art festival she wore a light blue T-shirt belted over a long skirt and pair of tan leather sandals. As we began chatting, I saw a stack of photos, probably a hundred or more, on a table next to her art. There were many pictures of horses, donkeys, sheep, cactus, and Native American women and children. Franny explained that she was the photographer and that she has been taking photographs for years. Her photos inspire her art. Franny was open and honest and we scheduled an interview. A few weeks later, I talked to Franny over the phone. The interview was as poignant as if she was sitting in the room with me.

Franny has experienced the most startling instances of unbidden intuition or premonitions that I have heard of. I use the term "unbidden intuition" to describe the use of intuition that is *not sought or asked for, but comes to reveal a precognitive event, to offer life-saving advice, or to understand immediately information about another person's life.* Franny shared with me this intense intuitive experience she had while visiting her acupuncturist's office. On the wall was a hand drawn, pretty black-and-white drawing of a Japanese woman in a kimono. To anyone else viewing this pen and ink drawing it was pleasant to look at. But Franny saw something else entirely:

I saw this woman screaming. I didn't see a pretty thing drawn, I saw an artist in her last moments, screaming …

Franny got up on the treatment table, looked over at the doctor and said matter-of-factly, "That woman is screaming in the drawing. Who did the drawing?"

My acupuncturist's face went white. We spent the next hour discussing what had happened. She told me the artist had been a patient. This woman had been killed in her vehicle due to a flood. There had been a flash flood in the area. She was in her car, had gotten swept down the street in her car. There was a failed rescue attempt and she ended up drowning inside her car.

Franny saw, within the painting, the woman's last moments alive. After that, her acupuncturist called her one of her "Intuitive Others."

Another intense episode of unbidden intuition occurred when Franny was a passenger in a car. She and her friends were driving to an artist reception in the rural area of their community. Franny looked out the car window and was shocked to see a man dragging a burning, flaming Christmas tree out the front door of his house:

I said to my friends in the car, "Did you see that?" They all just looked at me and no one said anything. No one saw anything. I was the only one who had seen the man running out his front door with a Christmas tree. My friends all looked at me like I was nuts.

I looked in the paper that Sunday thinking I would see something. I checked Monday, nothing. Then in Tuesday's paper there was a huge photograph of this man whose face had been burned, with a large headline: "Burning Christmas Tree Hurts Man—He Drags It Out to Save Home."

Franny witnessed an event that had yet to happen: it was the same house she had driven by on Saturday night, but the event happened on Sunday.

Franny's first instance of premonitions happened when she was seventeen years old. Franny was raised in the hot desert of the southwest. One evening, driving alone in the car in a rural unpopulated neighborhood, she stopped at a four-way intersection with a light that had just turned red:

I was sitting at a T in the road about to make a left turn. Instead of going when the light turned, I heard a voice inside of me say, "You had better stay." I sat through the light. Someone came speeding through the light on their red. I was stunned. If I had gone I would have been nailed on the driver's door. That was when I really started to pay attention to the voice—it wasn't an inner voice, it was a voice from somewhere else.

Franny's mother raised her on her own. No other relatives were in the immediate area, and her father was absent from her life until much later. Her mother was not intuitive to Franny's recollection, but she did take Franny to Native American events almost every weekend when she was a child. The Tohono O'odham Nation extended around their small community in the southwest, and that is where she spent time with her mother many afternoons while she was growing up. Franny remembers:

I loved seeing the Native American women riding the bus. They looked to me like they were playing dress-up with the earrings, jewelry, moccasins, and long skirts in velvet. Their hair was beautiful. I was in awe. That was the start of it. Because I was in the 4-H, I got very, very close to my animals like many Native Americans, and even now, I feel more comfortable in a Native American setting than in an Anglo setting.

In 1971, Franny had what she calls a "defining moment in life." She went to a batik art demonstration and was immediately fascinated and compelled to create it herself. She bought a book of Batik art along with some art supplies and taught herself. After the batik demonstration, Franny focused completely on batik and stopped working in clay and print blocking. Batik is an art form that dates back to Egypt and is over 3,000 years old. When modern archaeologists explored the pyramids and the tombs there, they found batik art nestled among other treasures. Franny begins her artwork with a white piece of fabric. She draws on the fabric her sketch with all of the details. She can adjust the drawing, but mostly it is a complete drawing and how she envisions the painting:

> *Batik is a way of painting on fabric with the painting part done with wax. I use hot bees wax with a tool—a brush with little spouts. The wax goes through the fabric and adheres to the fabric. Then I add the dyes, which are pure pigments from Europe. There are layers and layers of wax and color. I imagine a living image for the work—I'm interested in movement and the human body and all animals and how they move. I use color to enhance movement.*

Franny sees her art and intuition that guides her as one and the same. She has never tried to conceal her intuition. In her everyday life, her intuition is noticeable, and when she has intuitive moments, it has the potential to startle other people. Words and ideas pop right out of her mouth.

Franny's health took a dramatic turn when she was diagnosed with uterine cancer at the age of fifty. She was devastated, but said that she finally knew what was wrong with her, and that she had hope for getting better. After she was diagnosed with cancer, Franny remembers a lovely warm Christmas day, when her house was filled with family and friends. Franny said she was not feeling well, but was thrilled for her daughter's college graduation and upcoming marriage. Her father had recently come back into Franny's life after his fourth wife had passed away, and he was at her house as well. They were getting ready for dinner when a man wearing a backpack knocked at the door. He asked

Franny if he could paint the house numbers on the curb in front of the house. He said he had been painting the numbers in the neighborhood and could he do hers as well. Franny thought it was curious he was working on Christmas Day, but said, "Sure, you can paint them." After he finished, he came back to the door and Franny then invited him to join their family for Christmas dinner. He declined, said he wasn't dressed or clean enough for dinner, but Franny offered to bring him a meal away from the people on her front porch. He accepted, ate the meal, thanked Franny then went on his way.

Months passed.

Franny was put under a treatment plan for her cancer. One afternoon while she was napping on the couch, someone knocked on the door. The man from Christmas day appeared at her door again. Franny answered the door, and the man said:

"I wanted to ask you if I could use you for a job reference? Things are improving for me and I have a chance of getting a job if I could use your name as a reference. Do you remember I painted your house numbers on your curb on Christmas Day?"

Franny asked him how he remembered her house again. He said:

"Oh, I would never forget someone who had given me dinner on Christmas."

Then, the man's backpack appeared in her mind. She remembered he had told her when he painted the curb his supplies were in the backpack, but she had never seen him take out any supplies. Her body began to tingle and got warm all over from head to toe. She knew, in that second, that everything with her cancer was going to be okay. She realized who this man was:

When he left I realized why he had a backpack on. To conceal his wings!! He was an Angel!

Franny's encounter with an Angel left no doubt in her mind that her health would recover and she would be cancer free. Her ability to use her intuition daily and act upon it has led to a life full of creative expression that she shares with everyone around her. Each day has been a gift to her that she uses to create from her soul the aspects of Native American life that have moved her since she was a child visiting the Tohono O'odham Nation.

Her premonitions or unbidden intuitions are a natural occurrence in her life, and Franny has come to terms with this unique aspect of herself. She has come to rely on the voice inside of her and listens deeply for the guidance that sustains her well-being. Franny says in parting about her life:

Intuition just happens, I don't focus on it, but it's always there. Intuition guides my art painted on canvas.

CHAPTER TEN

Ellen & Liz—Sisters of the Heart

~~

*When I see Liz, I see the father caring for the flocks of
children and animals when she is doing what she does.
I see the mother who cares for the children. I see the
hugeness of Liz. Even though I'm the oldest,
I've always felt she is sort of the big sister.
I think of her as a big heart.
Ellen and Liz*

Ellen and Liz are sisters of the heart. I met them both at a book club I had joined in Flagstaff a few years ago. I was so struck when I met them by the kindness and love for others they radiated, and for the deep, abiding love and respect they had for each other. I asked if they would be interested in being interviewed on their feelings about intuition and their own life journeys. I was thrilled when they agreed. We met on a cold blustery day at my house and settled down with our tea to discuss life. Both women had had long careers in the corporate world, retired from them and are active in a number of different ventures. They work at a local real estate agency as realtors, specializing in the needs of seniors. Liz started a new business, *Golden Years*, a concierge service providing seniors and their families holistic and compassionate day-to-day life services, as well as moving management to help seniors transition to smaller living communities. She works tirelessly raising money for animal causes. Ellen created a new business as well, *First Move*, a way to help people cultivate peace in everyday life. She wants to "inspire others to realize the basic goodness inherent in each one of us." They are also deeply committed to a spiritual path that has been unfolding throughout their lives with various teachers. I had heard from friends that both women had taken several trips to Brazil and had been training with a Brazilian shaman. What did they do with this work I wanted to know?

Liz had gone to Brazil on her first trip with a friend more or less to go and see what it was all about. She met Henrique there, a shaman teaching people about healing and Mandala work. She said she felt a little intimidated, and on the first day was the last person to enter in the room. Liz was taking notes for her friend Ann, and Henrique told her he was concerned at first because he wasn't able to get a read on her, then when she started writing, everything opened up around her. He said he saw so many interesting things, and said her mentors were higher than his. Liz learned to do healings there with the Brazilian group. She said a fear of hers going there was that she has always been deathly afraid of dying for whatever reason, of dying at a young age:

> We all did a healing to help us release our fears and I
> realized it's beautiful and ok to release those fears. What
> the community did in Brazil made sense to me and I

wanted to continue doing it! But, it didn't really speak to
my friend Ann. The healing done there is for individuals
and for the world. There is a little community there that
sits and prays for everything from the California earth-
quakes to the Seattle mudslides. I told Ellen she needed
to go here for her birthday and I knew she would like
it—all of the energy work.

Ellen told me the trip to Brazil didn't necessarily call to
her originally, but she had seen Liz shed her fear of death and
that she was peaceful. The community there was indeed special, a place of love and service. When she saw the powerful
transformational change in her sister, she knew Brazil and this
community would be a soulful experience. Ellen said she felt
performance anxiety about going there—feelings of not knowing exactly what you're doing, and feelings about other people
knowing more than she did who were better at this type of work
than herself. Henrique helped change that for her:

You can do healing yourself, he told me. Think of the
whole pantheon of self-help books. There is always
somebody else to tell you how to fix yourself, there are
basically 500 ways to fix yourself, countless ways to "fix"
yourself! He teaches you that there is nothing wrong
with you, and gives you information to see for your-
self, how to do this with energy work, and how to be
your highest self. Everybody has a mission, and mission
doesn't necessarily mean it's your job to save the plan-
et singlehandedly. Your mission could be to raise your

daughter to be who she is. "What I've learned, is that we have many missions in a lifetime, it's not just one role. This is another thing we get hung up on—the question of, 'What am I here to do?' We may have more missions than one. One of mine is to be here for the grandchildren in my family to act as a balance point for them, a different way to be for them. I think we are here to evolve as a species, to evolve our consciousness. All the things that we've done to get ourselves to this point served us really well, but they're not working so well now. The only way to change that is to shift our consciousness—what it means to be in relationship with each other, what it means to be in relationship to the planet, to Earth.

One of the healing modalities that both Ellen and Liz do together is with Mandalas. Mandalas are usually graphic symbols representing the universe in the shape of a circle with various symbols within it. The purpose is manifold: a living prayer, to promote healing, celebrate unions, or encourage new ways of thinking or transformations within yourself. They learned from their work in Brazil with Henrique how to create Mandalas with flowers, drawing images, using chalk, water, and candles for any blessing or healing ceremonies. Liz tells me that the images she draws during a Mandala ceremony are transmissions of what needs to be out there:

I see it as a prayer. You set your intentions and the images just come. The images that we draw represent the energies for the understanding of what is asking to be brought forth. There is trust. Using the flowers in the Mandala in Brazil you must be initiates into the community. It creates a way for people to come together and to honor the person for the Mandala. It is very, very powerful.

I've had the honor to participate in Mandala ceremonies with Liz and Ellen and have found it to be a potent, transformative experience. People are invited to the ceremony and bring flowers. All of the flowers are laid together off to one side. The Mandala is drawn on the ground by Liz and Ellen and filled in with drawings they are guided to create, with small candles floating in glass bowls of water, and a number of other objects. People place any flowers that they feel drawn to on the Mandala on the ground and the end result resembles a large living flower pulsating with life and sacred intention. The energy and love pouring from the flowers is peaceful and dynamic at the same time. The Mandala creates a way for people to honor the person or people for the Mandala. The Mandala work has become a significant blessing in Ellen's life:

We say the prayer, we draw the prayer, we activate the prayer by the lighting of the candles, activating the energies. It's talking to nature and the portals—all are one working together. I find working with the Mandalas transformative work. We ask people to come to the Mandala ceremony and through the participation in the process I see people being changed.

They also do long distance healing work with the Mandala ceremonies. On one occasion, they were asked to do a long distance healing on a man. In the room where they were praying they had turned off all the lights, and Ellen remembers her hand on its own accord rising to her throat during the healing. There were things in this man's throat that she was feeling that needed to be healed:

It's about learning to trust, being willing to trust—you may not know or understand what is happening, and learning to not make meaning around it while you're doing the healing. Not to judge it. Just show up for it.

It seemed that the trips to Brazil created a profound impact on Liz and Ellen. Their lives became even more enriched from the Mandala work. The intuition, the knowing that is deep within us, was reawakened and made visible in their lives. Ellen said that of all the stories she's read regarding women's intuition, there seems to be something larger than intuition happening:

I think it's a willingness to open and to listen to the song of God that's coming through each person. Each one of us is expressing it in a completely unique and different way. It's not this thing called intuition for me. It's the song of God coming through each person and what we're doing to open to it. Maybe it's not God, but we're all being sung—Liz is one note and you're another note and I'm another note and we've been raised to not hear the song, or our note within the song. Up until we're may-

be five years old we're hearing our note and our place within the song. Then all this human stuff comes in and covers it all up … and then we start to not like it anymore and we dabble. People ask Lizzie to go somewhere, she goes. People ask me to go somewhere, I go. But, since we found teachers who teach us we have it all inside of us, that's when we started to change. Not by buying a bunch of books, not by signing up for a bunch of programs, but learning to trust that WE CAN HEAR THE SONG OURSELVES! More than intuition, it's the trusting themselves that helped women to listen to their own song, to be their own note.

That trust is an ongoing journey in all our lives. When we learn to trust with unconditional love, we allow ourselves to move into a greater expansion of what we know, see, and feel. We move into a living state of grace where all wisdom is accessible. We have an emotional understanding of ourselves where growth and change happen. Higher levels of consciousness and the power to co-create with the divine become our norm. The truth of who we are pulsates out and aligns with the deepest core of our integrity. Our higher states of awareness can act to draw others to us, and become more expansive themselves.

Through trusting in themselves and a willingness to expand into following a deep-seated passion to serve others, Liz and Ellen give back to the world of themselves and profound transformational healings. Their desire to work together and serve the highest good is an example of grace made visible through unconditional love.

SEVEN STRATEGIES TO AWAKEN
YOUR INTUITION

1. Acknowledge That You Have Intuition

You are born with intuition and it is your birthright to use it in your daily life. Your inner voice always has your best interest at heart.

2. Start to Use Your Intuition

When you feel, see or hear your intuition at work—pay attention and follow through with actions based on the guidance. The more you trust your intuition, the more opportunities become available to you.

3. Release the Past

Work to release the old ticker tape of thoughts that no longer serve you. Consider yourself free to create positive thoughts that support your well-being.

4. Honor Your Path

Wherever you are on your path honor yourself. It took great courage to get where you are today. Release the need to judge yourself.

5. Live an Authentic Life

Live the life you want to live, not the life someone else believes is best for you. No matter how well-intentioned others are, we are the only ones that know what is best for a meaningful life filled with joy and purpose.

6. Practice Gratitude

Being thankful for our lives opens us to even greater opportunities for expansion of self. Appreciate the family and friends in your life. Give thanks for your health. Delight in nature and animals. Send blessings to those invisible others that guide and love us.

7. Be Open to Change

Change happens every day and leaves room for new beginnings. We can make new choices for a unique life honoring the special gifts we bring to the world.

SUGGESTIONS FOR FURTHER READING

Alberdi, L. (2000). *Channeling: What It Is, and How To Do It*. Maine: Samuel Weiser, Inc.

Alexander, E. (2012). *Proof of Heaven—A Neurosurgeon's Journey Into the Afterlife*. New York. Simon & Shuster.

Anderson, R. & Vipassana, E. H. (2006). "Intuitive Inquiry: An Exploration of Embodiment Among Female Mystics." Fischer, Constance T. (Ed.), *Qualitative Research Methods for Psychologists*. pp. 301-330. San Diego, CA, US: Elsevier Academic Press.

Anderson, S.R. & Hopkins, P. (1991). *The Feminine Face of God*. New York: Bantam Books.

Baxter, L., & Babbie, E. (2004). *The Basics of Communication Research*. Belmont, CA: Wadsworth/Thomson Learning.

Bell, E. (2008). *Theories of Performance*. Los Angeles: Sage Publications.

Benthov, I. (1977). *Stalking the Wild Pendulum—On the Mechanics of Consciousness*. Rochester, Vermont. Destiny Books.

Bolen, J. (1994). *Crossing to Avalon – A Woman's Midlife Pilgrimage*. San Francisco: HarperSanFrancisco.

Bowman, C. (1997). *Children's Past Lives—How Past Lives Memories Affect Your Child*. New York. Bantam Books.

Brubaker, R. & Cooper. F. (2000). "Beyond 'identity.'" *Theory and Society* (29). pp. 1-47. Netherlands: Kluwer Academic Publishers.

Butler. J. (1993). *Bodies That Matter*. New York. Routledge.

Cameron, J. (1992). *The Artist's Way—A Spiritual Path to Higher Creativity*. New York: G.P. Putnam's Sons.

Coelho, P. (1998). *The Alchemist*. New York. HarperCollins.

Counsell, C. &Wolf, L. (2001). *Performance Analysis*. London: Routledge.

Duerk, J. (1989). *I Sit Listening to the Wind: Women's Encounter Within Herself*. Philadelphia. Innisfree Press.

Duerk, J. (1993). *Circle of Stones: Women's Journey to Herself*. Philadelphia, Pa. Innisfree Pres.

Estes, C. P. (1992). *Women Who Run With the Wolves*. New York. Random House.

Flinders, C.L. (1993). *Enduring Grace—Living Portraits of Seven Women Mystics*. New York: HarperCollins.

Giles, M. (1989). *The Feminist Mystic*. New York. Crossroad.

Goffman, E. (1959). *The Presentation of Self in Everyday Life*. New York: Anchor Books.

Goffman, E. (1963). *Stigma—Notes on the Management of Spoiled Identity*. Englewood Cliffs, New Jersey: Prentice-Hall, Inc.

Klaassen, J. (2001). "The Taint of Shame: Failure, Self-Distress, and Moral Growth." *Journal of Social Philosophy*. 32 (2), pp.174 -196.

Klimo, J. (1998). "Channeling: Investigations on Receiving Information" in *Journeys Out of the Body*. Monroe, R., ed. New York, New York: Doubleday.

Lachman, B. (1993). *The Journal of Hildegard of Bingen*. New York. Bell Tower.

Link, B. & Phelan, J. (2001). "Conceptualizing Stigma." *Annual Review of Sociology* (27). 363-385.

Moore, T. (1992). *Care of the Soul*. New York. HarperCollins.

Moorjani, A. (2012). *Dying to Be Me—My Journey From Cancer, To Near Death, To True Healing*. Carlsbad, CA. Hay House.

Myss, C. (1996). *Anatomy of Spirit: The Seven Stages of Power and Healing*. New York. Harmony Books/Crown Publishers.

Myss, C. (2003). *Sacred Contracts: Awakening Your Diving Potential*. New York. Three Rivers Press.

Newton, M. (2003). *Destiny of Souls—New Case Studies of Life Between Lives*. St. Paul: Llewellyn Publications.

Newton, M. (2003). *Journey of Souls—Case Studies of Life Between Lives*. St. Paul: Llewellyn Publications.

Pelias, Ronald J. (1992). *Performance Studies: The Interpretation of Aesthetic Texts*. New York: St. Martin's Press.

Peters. J. D. (1999). *Speaking Into the Air*. Chicago: The University of Chicago Press.

Pinel, E. C. (2004). "You're Just Saying That Because I'm a Woman: Stigma Consciousness and Attributions to Discrimination." *Self and Identity*, 3, 39-51.

Praugh, J. (1997). *Talking to Heaven A Medium's Message of Life After Death*. New York, New York: Dutton.

Praugh, J. (2001). *Heaven and Earth, Making the Psychic Connection.* New York, New York: Simon and Shuster Source.

Roman, S., & Parker, D. (1987). *Opening to Channel: How to Connect With Your Guide.* Tiburon, CA: H.J. Kramer, Inc.

Rubin, G. (2009). *The Happiness Project.* New York: Harper Collins.

Schulz, M. L. (1998). *Awakening Intuition.* New York: Three Rivers Press.

Schulz, M. L. (2005). *The New Feminine Brain: Developing Your Intuitive Genius.* New York: Free Press.

Shirely, D. & Langan-Fox, J. (1996). "Intuition: A Review of the Literature." *Psychological Reports,* 79, pp. 563-584.

Stone, M. (1976). *When God Was A Woman.* New York. Harcourt Brace.

Taylor, J. B. (2008). *My Stroke of Insight—A Brain Scientist's Personal Journey.* New York. Viking.

Tolle, E. (1997). *The Power of Now.* Toronto: Namaste Publishing.

Van Praugh, J. (2001). *Heaven and Earth—Making the Psychic Connection.* New York. Simon and Shuster Source.

Walsh, N.D. (1995). *Conversations With God.* Charlottesville: Hampton Roads Publishing Co.

Weiss, Br. (1988). *Many Lives, Many Masters—The True Story of a Prominent Psychiatrist, His Young Patient, and the Past-Life Therapy That Changed Their Lives.* New York. Simon & Shuster.

Williamson, M. (1994). *Illuminata: A Return to Prayer.* New York. Riverhead Books.

Woodman, M. (1993). *Leaving My Father's House—A Journey to Conscious Feminity*. Boston. Shambhala.

Zukov, G. (1990). *The Seat of the Soul*. New York: Fireside/Simon & Shuster.

ABOUT THE AUTHOR

An international speaker, author, intuitive, and yogi, Stephanie Petrie has presented intuitive readings for clients in the U.S., Europe, Egypt, Australia, and China, including Tibet. At the heart of her intuitive work lies a desire for others to attain happiness and meaning on their life journeys.

Stephanie earned a Bachelor of Arts from Gettysburg College and a Master of Arts in Communication from Northern Arizona University. Additionally, she's worked in the field of Educational Publishing as a Content, Curriculum, and Assessment Specialist for over 17 years.

She is the author of *Following the Signs: One Woman's Journey for Happiness, Meaning, and the Quest for a Spiritual Life.*